ROMANS
Alive in Christ

"I am not ashamed of the gospel, because it is the power
of God for the salvation of everyone
who believes: first for the Jew, then for the Gentile.
For in the gospel a righteousness from God is revealed,
a righteousness that is by faith from first to last,
just as it is written: 'The righteous will live by faith.' "
Romans 1:16–17

Compiled by David A. Lumpp

CPH.
SAINT LOUIS

Series editors: Thomas J. Doyle and Rodney L. Rathmann

We solicit your comments and suggestions concerning this material. Please write to Product Manager, Adult Bible Studies, Concordia Publishing House, 3558 S. Jefferson Avenue, St. Louis, MO 63118-3968.

4   5   6   7   8   9   10   05 04 03 02

Contents

A Brief Introduction to Romans

St. Paul's letter to the Romans is the first epistle in the New Testament because it is the longest, but it could also occupy that position because of the importance of its contents as well. It has always played an important role in the history of the church, because it summarizes so well the essential emphases of the apostle's evangelical theology. Martin Luther had an especially exalted view of Romans: "This epistle is really the chief part of the New Testament, and is truly the purest gospel. It is worthy not only that every Christian should know it word for word, by heart, but also that he should occupy himself with it every day, as the daily bread of the soul. We can never read it or ponder over it too much; for the more we deal with it, the more precious it becomes and the better it tastes." ("Preface to the Epistle of St. Paul to the Romans," from 1546, in *Luther's Works*, American Edition, vol. 35 [Philadelphia: Muhlenberg, 1960], p. 365.)

Romans summarizes a quarter century of Paul's missionary preaching and teaching. It was written from Corinth at the end of Paul's third missionary journey, probably in A.D. 56 or 57. This was a turning point in his life, for he planned to bring to a close his work among Christian congregations in Asia Minor and in eastern Europe and then turn his attention to a new field west of Rome. Before leaving, he wrote to the Romans the key aspects of the Gospel of God's mercy in Jesus Christ. Indeed, this explains why Romans is more comprehensive than Paul's other letters, for he was writing to introduce himself and the Gospel he preached to the Christians at Rome. It was his hope that they would support him with their prayers and offerings as he embarked on his new work in the west.

Throughout the letter Paul emphasizes that God's mercy comes to undeserving people who stand under the accusation and condemnation of the Law. In the Gospel of Jesus Christ, God freely gives righteousness to men and women through faith alone, and not on the basis of their own accomplishments or their own fastidious efforts to keep the Law. Paul insists that Jesus Christ is God's definitive Word, His final action, and thus is the fulfillment of all of God's promises. This unconditional promise is the sole basis of people's relationship with God.

It is the purpose of Romans to unfold some of its implications. Let's take a look at Romans and learn and grow!

Lesson 1

The Power of the Gospel (Romans 1)

Theme Verses

"I am not ashamed of the gospel, because it is the power of God for the salvation of everyone who believes: first for the Jew, then for the Gentile. For in the gospel a righteousness from God is revealed, a righteousness that is by faith from first to last, just as it is written: 'The righteous will live by faith' " (Romans 1:16–17).

Goal

We seek to understand how the righteousness of God is not so much about what God is in Himself or about what God asks of us, but about what He gives to us in the Gospel of Jesus Christ through faith.

What's Going On Here?

The apostle Paul begins his most comprehensive doctrinal letter with a summary of the Gospel he preached and with a statement of the basis of his calling to be an apostle to the Gentiles. This Gospel was promised in the Old Testament Scriptures (1:2–3). The resurrection of Jesus ratified Jesus' identity as Son of God and victorious Lord (1:4). Through this Gospel, Paul called his audience in Rome and elsewhere to "the obedience that comes from faith" (1:5). Those to whom he wrote—very likely to a community of Christians that included both Jews and Gentiles—were among those "called to belong to Jesus Christ" (1:6).

Verses 8–15 are part of Paul's hopes and plans to travel to Rome, where he had not visited before he wrote this letter. These verses are a model of pastoral concern: The Romans are in his prayers (1:10); he hopes for mutual encouragement in the faith (1:12); and he notes that his outreach and ministry is and will be universal, extending both to Gentiles and Jews alike (1:13–14).

Whatever his audience, his message and his gospel will be consistent. Paul was "eager to preach the gospel also to [those] who are at Rome" (1:15). Let's listen to that Gospel as Paul unfolds it in this letter.

Searching the Scriptures

1. How does Paul summarize the basic human situation that produces all of his problems (1:18)? What does it mean when Paul states that human beings are "godless"?

Hold the truth in Unrighteousness

27.28

2. What is the essential characteristic of idolatry? In what sense is idolatry the source of all other sins? See Romans 1:25.

who changed the truth of God into a lie and worshipped and served the creature more then the Creator.

3. What is the end result of persistent idolatry?

God gave them over to impurity Death.

4. Romans 1:22–32 is virtually a catalog of human sin and folly. Are the sins enumerated in these verses the cause or the consequence of our problem?

Consequence.

5. Does the "righteousness of God" as Paul uses the expression refer to

says in 1:16–17, how is the righteousness of God revealed to human
beings? _Ties then together._

Through his word.

6. How do human beings come to have the righteousness of God in their own lives? See Romans 1:17b.

The just shall live by faith.

7. Go back and read Romans 1:16 again. Why could Paul be so confident and emphatic about the Gospel? _It is the power of God._

The Word for Us

1. For whom was the Gospel that Paul preached intended? On what basis do human beings—all human beings—relate to God? What does that say about our own outreach?

Intended for all christians and non christians

2. In many ways these verses are about priorities, about what comes first and what will then follow. What is always of first importance to the Christian? On the basis of the verses read in this lesson, why and how is this a source of great comfort for the Christian?

Living by faith (Believing in the Gospel)
We are saved.

3. In our lesson and in the questions from the last section we have focused on the Law portions of this text before we turned to the Gospel. This reflects the pattern of Paul's outline of Romans. Why do you think that structural observation is significant?

The law condemns, the gospel saves. If you were not judged and condemned there would be no need for salvation.

Closing

Gracious God, we rejoice that You have given us the righteousness of Your Son in the Gospel. Assure us of Your abiding presence with us, and keep us ever mindful of Your consistent care for us and the mercy You hold out to us. In Jesus' name. Amen.

Righteousness Apart from Law (Romans 2:1–3:20)

3:1–20

Theme Verses

"A man is not a Jew if he is only one outwardly, nor is circumcision merely outward and physical. No, a man is a Jew if he is one inwardly; and circumcision is circumcision of the heart, by the Spirit, not by the written code. Such a man's praise is not from men, but from God" (Romans 2:28–29).

Goal

In this section from Romans we seek to realize that God's Law exposes the unrighteousness of all people, and that because of the impossibility of attaining righteousness by human behavior on the basis of Law, we are that much more driven to the mercy of God as our source of consolation and forgiveness.

What's Going On Here?

Just as the second half of Romans 1 described the sinfulness of the Gentiles, Romans 2 indicts the self-righteousness of much of Judaism and Romans 3:1–20 summarizes the guilt of human beings in general. Individual acts of disobedience or lawlessness are symptomatic of sin, which always threatens to be a dominating principle in human life. Given this universality to guilt, being "a Jew" in the sense of being part of the people of God (2:28–29) is a matter of faith and inner disposition. The Law will not help us here, for through the Law one becomes conscious of sin.

Searching the Scriptures

1. In the light of Paul's audience for this letter, what does he mean when he says in 2:1, "you who pass judgment do the same things"?

Judgement must also be applied to the judge. Hypocritical judgement - All stand condemned. look inwardly first

2. Read Romans 2:4. For what reason is God especially forbearing toward sinners?

Gods Kindness leads ynto repentnce.

Ezekial 33-11

3. How do 2:7–11 indicate that God does not show partiality? On what basis are some people condemned? Now go back and reread Romans 1:16–17 from Lesson 1. On what basis are people saved? Are Jews and Gentiles saved in different ways?

4. Read Romans 2:12–16. How do Gentiles, who do not have the Old Testament Law, know what is expected of them? What does it mean to "do by nature things required by the law"?

5. Read Romans 2:17–29. What is the basic point of these verses? How does Paul use the imagery of "circumcision" in verses 25–29?

6. Read Romans 3:1–20, especially verses 9–12. How do these verses make the same point Paul has been driving home throughout much of this first part of Romans?

7. The climax of this section is in 3:19–20. What is the inevitable outcome of a confrontation with God's Law?

God's Word for Us

1. Reread Romans 2:1. In what ways do we do at least some of the *kinds* of things that we condemn in others?

2. How do the readings from this section help inform our attitudes towards God's Law?

Closing

Merciful God, You have made us Your children through the circumcision of the heart, as Your Holy Spirit gives us faith to lay hold of Your promise. We give thanks for the forgiveness that You have freely imparted to us apart from the Law, and in this gift of Your forgiveness we rejoice. Amen.

Lesson 3

"Righteousness from God" (Romans 3:21–31)

Theme Verses

"This righteousness from God comes through faith in Jesus Christ to all who believe. There is no difference, for all have sinned and fall short of the glory of God, and are justified freely by His grace through the redemption that came by Christ Jesus. God presented Him as a sacrifice of atonement, through faith in His blood" (Romans 3:21–25a).

Goal

In this lesson we seek to understand the very essence of the Gospel message, namely, that purely out of His mercy God forgives us our sin and imparts to us the righteousness of Jesus Christ.

What's Going On Here?

Today's lesson from Romans 3:21–31 is one of several core theological chapters in Romans. In many ways it summarizes and pulls together some of the same "salvation" that have been anticipated in and scattered among the readings for the first two lessons. Righteousness of God comes not from Law, but is God's gift in Jesus Christ. The theme of justification by grace through faith is introduced as well, and this becomes central to the argument of this epistle thereafter.

Searching the Scriptures

1. We have now repeated several times that the righteousness of God is His gift in Jesus Christ. For Lutheran Christians this observation has historical as well as theological interest, because it was this biblical phrase—

"a righteousness from God"—that was so troublesome to the young Martin Luther. He was frightened by the concept, because he thought it was either a characteristic or a demand of God. Part of the problem arose because the same Latin word is used for righteousness and justice. He knew that God was righteous and just, and he feared that his own conduct was not righteous enough—hence, his understandable anxiety.

With this background in mind, how would the prepositions in verses 21 and 22 help Luther and others like him who may share his fear?

2. What do people have to do to enjoy this righteousness in their own lives?

3. What if someone asks, "Well, isn't believing a work?"

4. Read 3:23–24. Are there any differences in how some people are able to approach God?

5. Two new and crucial concepts are introduced in verse 24, "justification" and "redemption." While they are not defined explicitly in this verse, what can we say about both words just on the basis of what we read in verse 24?

6. "Justification" is a word from a legal context, while "redemption" reflects the language of the marketplace. Their use together reflects the fact that there is a variety of ways to describe what God has done for our salvation in Jesus Christ.

The legal nature of "justification" underscores for us that it is not about our improvement or about our becoming increasingly acceptable to God. "To justify" is to "declare not guilty" or to "pardon." Stated positively, it is to "declare righteous." This is God's pronouncement, God's declaration; and the pronouncement confers precisely what it promises.

We know from our own experience what it means "to redeem" something. It means to "buy back." In the ancient world, it usually referred to paying the redemption or ransom price to purchase freedom for a slave, so that his redemption was also his liberation.

On the basis of these verses, on what is our justification based and what is the price of human redemption?

7. Romans 3:25 refers to Jesus as a "sacrifice of atonement." What is the biblical background behind the use of this expression? What does it mean that Jesus is a sacrifice of atonement?

The Word for Us

1. In verse 30 Paul reminds his readers that "there is only one God." How does this indicate that there is no salvation apart from Jesus Christ, and what does this imply about our missionary privilege and responsibility?

2. How does the Gospel of Jesus Christ help us to see the Law in its true perspective and significance?

Closing

I trust, O Christ, in You alone;
    No earthly hope avails me.
You will not see me overthrown
    When Satan's host assails me.
No human strength, no earthly pow'r
    Can see me through the evil hour,
    For You alone my strength renew.
I cry to You!
    I trust, O Lord, Your promise true.

Confirm in us Your Gospel, Lord,
    Your promise of salvation.
And make us keen to hear Your Word
    And follow our vocation:
To spend our lives in love for You,
    To bear each other's burdens too.
    And then, at last, when death shall loom,
O Savior, come
    And bear Your loved ones safely home.

Lesson 4

Promise and Faith
(Romans 4)

Theme Verses

"Therefore, the promise comes by faith, so that it may be by grace and may be guaranteed to all Abraham's offspring—not only to those who are of the law but also to those who are of the faith of Abraham. He is the father of us all. As it is written: 'I have made you a father of many nations.' He is our father in the sight of God, in whom he believed—the God who gives life to the dead and calls things that are not as though they were" (Romans 4:16–17).

Goal

We seek to recognize that the promise of God comes before and apart from any works we might perform. Indeed, this is what grace is about: God addressing the unworthy—the ungodly—with His pardon.

What's Going On Here?

Romans 4 is crucial to the argument of Romans. It is a retelling of the story of Abraham in the context of God's unfolding of His plan of salvation. It is crucial because of the place Abraham enjoyed in the rabbinic tradition of the time. In Jewish literature contemporary to the time of St. Paul, it was said that Abraham had accumulated so much merit that Jews in later periods could draw on it for themselves.

Given this popular tradition, Paul had to show that not even Abraham was justified by his works. God's gracious action in Christ was consistent with the way He had acted with Abraham. Thus, Romans 4 argues that Abraham was justified through faith—apart from works, circumcision, and Law.

If this is the case with Abraham, it is certainly the case with us today as well.

Searching the Scriptures

1. Read Romans 4:4–5. How do these verses underscore the free and undeserved nature of God's grace?

2. Read Romans 4:11. What was the significance of Abraham's circumcision?

3. How does Abraham's story as recounted in chapter 4 make the same point as earlier chapters about the extent of God's mercy and about the means by which human beings are saved?

4. Romans 4:3–4, and 22–23 use a form of the expression "credited ... as righteousness" (quoting Genesis 15:6 several times). How does this relate to the meaning of "justification" as that term was used in connection with chapter 3?

5. Romans 4:25 is both a summary of what has gone before and a thematic verse for the entire book. In fact, some scholars believe that Paul is here quoting from an early Christian confession. How does the verse use Jesus' crucifixion and His resurrection both to highlight the futility of human efforts to attain righteousness and the certainty of God's saving act in Jesus Christ?

The Word for Us

1. How is a life by faith and a life lived by the Law a contradiction? How are they mutually exclusive?

2. On the basis of the material in this chapter, how might we respond to those who despair of their attempts to "live a Christian life" and as a result wonder how God could possibly be favorably disposed to them?

Closing

He is arisen! Glorious word!
    Now reconciled is God, my Lord;
    The gates of heav'n are open.
My Jesus did triumphant die,
    And Satan's arrows broken lie,
    Destroyed hell's fiercest weapon.
Oh, hear
What cheer!
    Christ victorious,
    Rising glorious,
    Life is giving.
He was dead but now is living!

Lesson 5

Adam versus Christ (Romans 5)

Theme Verses

"For if, by the trespass of one man, death reigned through that one man, how much more will those who receive God's abundant provision of grace and of the gift of righteousness reign in life through the one man, Jesus Christ" (Romans 5:17).

Goal

We seek to recognize how Jesus Christ brings forgiveness, life, and peace to descendants of Adam, whose sin renders us hostile to God and would otherwise lead to our condemnation and death. God's grace in Christ overcomes Adam's sin—and ours.

What's Going On Here?

Romans 5 unfolds the many blessings that come with God's justification of the sinner, among them peace, joy, and the Holy Spirit. Paul contrasts an unbeliever's position in Adam, whose sin brings judgment and death, with the believer's status in Jesus Christ, whose death and resurrection brings righteousness and eternal life.

Searching the Scriptures

1. What is the significance of "peace with God" as introduced in Romans 5:1?

2. Verses 2, 4, and 5 of chapter 5 mention "hope." Why is our hope certain? On what is this hope based? On the basis of verse 5, how are we reminded of this certain hope?

3. Romans 5:6, 8, 10 makes a similar point to the one Paul made in Romans 4:5, namely, that everything that God gives us in Jesus Christ is entirely unmerited. The verses in Romans 5 effectively elaborate on Romans 4:5 in several ways. In what ways does Paul assert the extent of human need in these verses? What is the cumulative effect of these verses?

4. In verses 10 and 11 Paul introduces yet another word, reconciliation, to describe what happens through the Gospel (he had earlier talked about justification and redemption). Is reconciliation potential or actual?

5. In Romans 5:12 Paul begins a comparison between Adam, and the consequences of his sin, and Jesus, and the consequences of His saving work. To whom do the consequences of Adam's sin extend? To whom do the consequences of Jesus' saving act extend? See especially verses 12, 15–19 in connection with the sin of Adam; and verses 15–19 in connection with the act of Christ.

6. How does verse 20b underscore the magnitude and extent of God's grace?

The Word for Us

1. We have been justified, redeemed, and reconciled to God. Why is the past tense of the verb a source of great confidence for Christians?

2. Amid all of the great truths about our salvation described in Romans 5, Paul does refer to "our sufferings" in verse 3. What does such a mention in this context imply? How does the Gospel address this situation?

Closing

Salvation unto us has come
    By God's free grace and favor;
Good works cannot avert our doom,
    They help and save us never.
Faith looks to Jesus Christ alone,
Who did for all the world atone;
    He is our one Redeemer.

Since Christ has full atonement made
    And brought to us salvation,
Each Christian therefore may be glad
    And build on this foundation.
Your grace alone, dear Lord, I plead,
Your death is now my life indeed,
    For You have paid my ransom.

All blessing, honor, thanks, and praise
    To Father, Son, and Spirit,
The God who saved us by His grace;
    All glory to His merit.
O triune God in heav'n above,
You have revealed Your saving love;
    Your blessed name we hallow.

Lesson 6

Baptism, Death, and Resurrection (Romans 6)

Theme Verses

"Don't you know that all of us who were baptized into Christ Jesus were baptized into His death? We were therefore buried with Him through baptism into death in order that, just as Christ was raised from the dead through the glory of the Father, we too may live a new life" (Romans 6:3–4).

Goal

Through this chapter of Romans we seek to appreciate how our Baptism into Christ's death and resurrection is both the motivation for our new life of faith and freedom, and the source of our certainty of eternal life with the God who has spared nothing to save us.

What's Going On Here?

In Romans 3–5 Paul has unfolded God's plan for and accomplishment of our justification and redemption through the death and resurrection of Jesus Christ. Having been reconciled to God through Jesus' own sacrifice for our sin, Paul now explains the results of this new status. In the Gospel we receive the righteousness of Jesus Christ through faith. Our new life has begun!

Searching the Scriptures

1. Paul begins in verse 1 with a rhetorical question: "Shall we go on sinning so that grace may increase?" He responds with a very emphatic "By

no means!", which is sometimes also translated "God forbid!" What is the basis of this response from Paul? (See especially vv. 3–4.)

2. In Romans 6:4–11 does Paul refer to resurrection as a present or future event, or both?

3. How do verses 11 and 14b provide the context and interpretation for the apostle's directives in verses 12–13?

4. What is the point of Paul's use of the expression "wholeheartedly obeyed" in verse 17?

5. Note the crucial distinction in verse 23 between "wages" and "gift." How does this distinction underscore the central difference between Law and Gospel, and, for that matter, the nature of Christianity itself?

The Word for Us

1. How would you respond to someone who had heard the Gospel message and then asked, "Well, what about keeping the Ten Commandments? We must have to do something, don't we?"

2. In general, what is the significance of Paul's consistent use of the word *sin* in the singular, rather than using the plural *sins*? What difference might this make for your understanding of the Christian life?

3. In the 16th century Martin Luther derived great comfort in the face of temptation from his Baptism. On the basis of Romans 6, why and how do you think Baptism was able to provide such a strong spiritual resource for him? What about for you?

Closing

All who believe and are baptized
    Shall see the Lord's salvation;
Baptized into the death of Christ,
    They are a new creation;
Through Christ's redemption they will stand
Among the glorious heav'nly band
    Of ev'ry tribe and nation.

With one accord, O God, we pray,
    Grant us Your Holy Spirit;
Help us in our infirmity
    Through Jesus' blood and merit;
Grant us to grow in grace each day
By holy Baptism that we may
    Eternal life inherit.

Lesson 7

The Struggle Within (Romans 7)

Theme Verses

"So, my brothers, you also died to the law through the body of Christ, that you might belong to another, to Him who was raised from the dead, in order that we might bear fruit to God. For when we were controlled by our sinful nature, the sinful passions aroused by the law were at work in our bodies, so that we bore fruit for death. But now, by dying to what once bound us, we have been released from the law so that we serve in the new way of the Spirit, and not in the old way of the written code" (Romans 7:4–6).

Goal

In the face of the persistent struggle we face with sin and its consequences, we seek to claim for ourselves the accomplished fact that in Jesus Christ and in our Baptism we have died to sin and to the ever-accusing law. We now live a new life that He has given us, and we live for the new life that is ours in the Spirit.

What's Going On Here?

This chapter is often regarded as one of the most difficult in all of Paul's letters. It describes our life-and-death struggle with sin and the law, and it underscores the all-important fact that only by relating to God on the basis of the rescue He has provided in Jesus Christ—and not on the basis of our futile attempts to fulfill the law—is there any hope for an escape from the sin that enslaves us and the death to which sin leads. It is precisely this rescue that God has accomplished in the death and resurrection of His Son. This does not always remove or lessen the struggle, but it does assure us that the outcome depends not on us but on God who has and does keep His promises.

Searching the Scriptures

1. How does Romans 7:6 follow logically on the points Paul made in Romans 6:2–7?

2. In verses 7–13 of chapter 7 how does Paul contrast the nature of the law itself with what it does in practice?

3. What does it mean to be "sold as a slave to sin" (7:14) or to be "a prisoner of the law of sin" (7:23)?

4. Paul vividly describes his present situation in 7:21b–23, especially verse 23. How does the apostle describe "another law"?

5. Note the Law/Gospel juxtaposition in 7:24, 25. What point is Paul trying to make through this sharp contrast?

The Word for Us

1. Christians have long debated whether Paul is talking about his life before or after his conversion. What do you think? What is some of the evidence you might give from this chapter?

2. When the temptations of sin entice us, what promise can we claim?

3. The inner conflict described in this chapter is obviously intense. Is it more or less so for a Christian? Why?

Closing

Gracious God, we are assailed by the accusation of the Law, which incessantly exposes the sin in which we are mired. Assure us of the Gospel of Your Son's death and resurrection for us. Keep us mindful of the forgiveness that You continually hold out to us. Remind us that in Baptism we have become Your adopted children, and that You will not let us go. Amen.

Lesson 8

No Condemnation (Romans 8)

Theme Verses

"What, then, shall we say in response to this? If God is for us, who can be against us? He who did not spare His own Son, but gave Him up for us all—how will He not also, along with Him, graciously give us all things? Who will bring any charge against those whom God has chosen? It is God who justifies. Who is He that condemns? Christ Jesus, who died—more than that, who was raised to life—is at the right hand of God and is also interceding for us" (Romans 8:31–34).

Goal

Through this great Gospel chapter we seek to be reassured that God's message of forgiveness in Jesus Christ is always His definitive word to the troubled sinner. God's promise to us is so strong and powerful that nothing can separate us from His love demonstrated in the death and resurrection of Jesus.

What's Going On Here?

Romans 8 comes on the heels of the struggles and pathos depicted in Romans 7. There is only one response to the kind of spiritual warfare described in chapter 7, and that is the unconditional Gospel of Jesus Christ unfolded in chapter 8, which decisively silences the accusation of Law and overcomes the assaults of sin and death. We are more than conquerors, Paul observes, because if Jesus Christ is for us nothing can be against us.

Searching the Scriptures

1. Read Romans 8:1. What is the significance of this verse in the light of the struggle depicted in Romans 7?

2. What does Paul tell us about Jesus by saying in verse 3 that He was sent "in the likeness of sinful man." See also John 1:1, 14; Hebrews 4:14–16.

3. Twice in Romans 8:11 Paul assures his readers that they have the Holy Spirit living in them. Later, in verse 23, he says that we have the "first-fruits of the Spirit." In 1 Corinthians 6:19–20, written in roughly the same time frame as Romans, Paul makes a similar point. According to these verses, what are some of the implications of the Holy Spirit living within us? How might we honor God with our bodies?

4. Romans 8:29–30 celebrate God's predestining of His people to eternal salvation. Read these verses carefully and note all of the saving acts entailed by God's elective love. You may wish to consult some other related texts as well: Psalm 139:15–16; Ephesians 1:4–5; 1 Corinthians 1:9; Romans 5:1; and Philippians 3:21.

5. Because of Jesus' sacrifice on our behalf, no one can condemn Christians any longer. What actions of Jesus are presented by Paul in Romans 8:34 as evidence that we are free from condemnation?

The Word for Us

1. How is thinking about the true humanity of Jesus a source of comfort to us?

2. In Romans 8:12 Paul notes that he and his readers—then and now—have an obligation (see also 1:14). What is that obligation, and on what is it based?

3. The world and its problems often cause us to be afraid. According to Romans 8:15, what is our antidote to fear? See also 1 John 4:18.

4. How is God's predestining His children to salvation through the work of Jesus Christ a source of great comfort for Christians?

Closing

To God the Holy Spirit let us pray
      Most of all for faith upon our way
That He may defend us when life is ending
      And from exile home we are wending.
Lord, have mercy!

Transcendent Comfort in our ev'ry need,
      Help us neither scorn nor death to heed
That we may not falter nor courage fail us
      When the foe shall taunt and assail us.
Lord, have mercy!

Shine in our hearts, O Spirit, precious light;
      Teach us Jesus Christ to know aright
That we may abide in the Lord who bought us,
      Till to our true home He has brought us.
Lord, have mercy!

Lesson 9

Jesus Christ—The End of the Law (Romans 9–10)

Theme Verses

"If you confess with your mouth, 'Jesus is Lord,' and believe in your heart that God raised Him from the dead, you will be saved. For it is with your heart that you believe and are justified, and it is with your mouth that you confess and are saved. As the Scripture says, 'Anyone who trusts in Him will never be put to shame.' For there is no difference between Jew and Gentile—the same Lord is Lord of all and richly blesses all who call on Him, for, 'Everyone who calls on the name of the Lord will be saved'" (Romans 10:9–13).

Goal

We seek through the study of these two chapters to appreciate more fully God's patience with those who resist Him, and above all to acknowledge the surpassing character of God's mercy as it is extended to people who can of themselves make no claim upon it. We rejoice in the mercy He shows to us and to all people in Jesus, the Messiah, who is Himself the fulfillment of all God's promises and the one who brings the condemnation and accusation of the Law to an end.

What's Going On Here?

When many Israelites failed to receive Jesus as their Messiah, it was not because God's Word failed or because God was unjust, but because their hearts were hardened in their unbelief. Nevertheless, God persisted in bringing His mercy to the world through Israel.

Since no one becomes righteous before God by keeping the Law, God provided another way to obtain righteousness, namely, through faith in the Gospel—Jesus, our Savior. Though this Gospel had been proclaimed to Israel, most Israelites refused to receive it and claimed their own way of righteousness through the Law.

Searching the Scriptures

1. Paul always remembered the spiritual privileges given to Israel as God's chosen people. Eight of those privileges are noted in Romans 9:4–5. List them. Some other helpful background texts are: Genesis 15:17–21; 17:1–8; 22:15–18; Exodus 4:22; 16:10; 20:1–21; Isaiah 9:6–7; Matthew 1:2–16; Hebrews 9:1; 11:8–10.

2. Review Romans 9:14–21. Paul asks if God is unfair in choosing Isaac over Ishmael and Jacob over Esau. Think about it: If God acted "fairly," or strictly on the basis of justice, whom would He choose? See also Romans 3:10–21; 6:23. In fact, on what basis does God choose to deal with us (Romans 9:15–16)?

3. In Romans 9:22–29 Paul discusses God's great patience with Israel. Why was God so patient with Israel, despite His wrath? See especially verses 23–24; a clue is in the quotations from Hosea and Isaiah in verses 25–29.

4. How did Israel attempt to obtain righteousness? See Romans 9:32. What was wrong with attempting to obtain righteousness in this way? Look back to Romans 3:19–20.

5. If the Gentiles did not pursue righteousness, then how did they obtain it? See Ephesians 2:1–5, 8–9.

6. How does Romans 10:4 summarize not only much of this section but also much of the entire book of Romans as well?

7. Read Romans 10:6–7. What two things has God made unnecessary through the Gospel? Why are they unnecessary?

The Word for Us

1. As Paul considers his unsaved kinspeople, he offers a model for our response to those who do not know Jesus Christ. See Romans 10:1, what are his responses and how might we learn from them?

2. Paul's declaration that before God Jews and Gentiles are on the same footing (Romans 10:12) would have struck many as radical, even revolutionary. Read Galatians 3:26–29 for an indication of what other distinctions disappear when we consider our standing before God. How should this realization affect the way we relate to one another in our churches? See also James 2:1–17.

3. According to Romans 10:17 how does God give faith to people? What does this verse suggest to us about the importance of preaching, teaching, and personal confession of faith in bringing people to faith in Jesus Christ?

Closing

Dear Jesus, You only are the way, the truth, and the life. We thank and praise You because You have revealed Yourself to us and have given us new life and a certain hope for eternity. Use us to guide others to the way of righteousness that You have provided through Your death and resurrection for us and for all people. Amen.

Lesson 10

The Remnant and "All Israel" (Romans 11)

Theme Verses

"So too, at the present time there is a remnant chosen by grace. And if by grace, then it is no longer by works; if it were, grace would no longer be grace" (Romans 11:5–6).

Goal

We seek through a study of this chapter to recognize the new, spiritual "Israel" not as an ethnic or national entity, but as a community of faith, comprised of believing Jews and Gentiles, who both enter the family of God on the basis of His free, unconditional mercy expressed in Jesus Christ.

What's Going On Here?

In this chapter, along with chapters 9 and 10, Paul emphasizes that salvation comes to Jew and Gentile alike by God's mercy in Jesus Christ, who is the personal fulfillment of the promise to Abraham and to the rest of the patriarchs. On the one hand, there is no room for arrogance, for no one can claim God's favor as a right, or as something deserved. On the other hand, one stands outside of God's favor only because of unbelief, a rejection of God's free promise, and, correspondingly, because of a misguided reliance on works of Law. Together, the believing remnant of Jews and Gentiles who lay hold of this promise through faith comprise the new Israel of God.

Searching the Scriptures

1. Read Romans 11:1–6. Most Israelites had rejected the Messiah whom God had sent. But God did not reject His people. What proof does Paul offer that God had not rejected Israel?

2. In Romans 11:1–6 Paul refers to the 7000 Israelites in the time of Elijah who had remained faithful to God, and he affirms a "remnant chosen by grace" (v. 5) in his own time. Who would be considered the remnant within Israel during the time of Paul? See also Acts 2:5, 36–41.

3. Paul says that Israel stumbled over the "stumbling stone" (Romans 9:32–33), but they did not fall beyond recovery. In other words, what hope does Paul still hold out for those Jews who had rejected Christ?

4. In Romans 11:17–24 Paul presents the vivid image of the cultivated olive tree and the wild olive shoot. What does the cultivated olive tree represent? For background help, see also Jeremiah 11:16–17 and Hosea 14:6–7.

5. What does "all Israel will be saved" (in v. 26) mean? As you wrestle with this question, read Romans 2:28–29; 4:9–12; 9:6–8; Galatians 6:15–16; Ephesians 2:11–13, 19–22; and 1 Peter 2:9–10.

God's Word for Us

1. What does Paul's attitude suggest to us when our attempts to share the Gospel with someone are rebuffed?

2. Looking back over Romans 9–11, what common themes run through the three chapters, and how do these themes inform our daily Christian lives?

Closing

The God of Abr'am praise,
>Who reigns enthroned above;
Ancient of everlasting days
>And God of love.
Jehovah, great I Am!
>By earth and heav'n confessed;
I bow and bless the sacred name
>Forever blest.

The God of Abr'am praise,
>Whose all-sufficient grace
Shall guide me in my pilgrim days
>In all my ways.
He deigns to call me friend;
>He calls Himself my God.
And He shall save me to the end
>Through Jesus' blood.

He by Himself has sworn;
>I on His oath depend.
I shall, on eagle wings upborne,
>To heav'n ascend.
I shall behold His face;
>I shall His pow'r adore
And sing the wonders of His grace
>Forevermore.

Lesson 11

Living Sacrifices
(Romans 12)

Theme Verses

"Therefore, I urge you, brothers, in view of God's mercy, to offer your bodies as living sacrifices, holy and pleasing to God—this is your spiritual act of worship. Do not conform any longer to the pattern of this world, but be transformed by the renewing of your mind. Then you will be able to test and approve what God's will is—His good, pleasing and perfect will" (Romans 12:1–2).

Goal

We seek through this chapter to recognize that the Gospel is our only motive for sanctified living, and that the context for providing mutual support for our lives of praise and service is the Christian church, the body of Christ.

What's Going On Here?

In Romans 12 Paul brings us to the "therefore" that follows inevitably from his unfolding of the Gospel in the first 11 chapters. Paul is putting to work in the Christian life the spiritual truths that he has developed to this point. The setting for this development is the Christian community, here described as the body of Christ with Jesus at its head. In this community we use our gifts for service and sacrifice, not self-aggrandizement.

Searching the Scriptures

1. In verse 1 Paul urges his readers "to offer your bodies as living sacrifices." What motivation does Paul offer for doing this? See especially verse 1a and also 1 John 4:19.

2. Throughout this chapter Paul exhorts his readers to work together with and get along with each other. On the basis of verse 4–8, what is the theological basis for making this point?

3. What is the connection between the character traits Paul identifies in verse 12: "Be joyful in hope, patient in affliction, faithful in prayer"?

4. Paul speaks of living at peace with everyone in verse 18. What two conditions precede this imperative?

5. In verse 20 Paul quotes Proverbs 25:21–22 to show the impact of overcoming evil with good? What is the apostle's point here? What does he mean by the phrase, "You will heap burning coals on his head"?

The Word for Us

1. What does it mean for us that God's will is described in verse 2 as being "good," "pleasing," and "perfect"?

2. Romans 12:2 gives three directives to be implemented in our daily lives: "Do not conform any longer to the pattern of this world"; "Be transformed by the renewing of your mind"; and "Test and approve what God's will is." How can each directive be followed in our own circumstances?

3. How might the overall teaching of this chapter be applied to our life together in the fellowship of the Christian church?

Closing

O Jesus, I have promised
    To serve Thee to the end;
Be Thou forever near me,
    My Master and my Friend;
I shall not fear the battle
    If Thou art by my side,
Nor wander from the pathway
    If Thou wilt by my Guide.

Oh, let me feel Thee near me,
    The world is ever near;
I see the sights that dazzle,
    The tempting sounds I hear.
My foes are ever near me,
    Around me and within;
But, Jesus, draw Thou nearer,
    And shield my soul from sin.

O Jesus, Thou hast promised
    To all who follow Thee
That where Thou art in glory
    There shall Thy servant be;
And, Jesus, I have promised
    To serve Thee to the end;
Oh, give me grace to follow,
    My Savior and my Friend.

Lesson 12

Submission and Love
(Romans 13)

Theme Verses

"Everyone must submit himself to the governing authorities, for there is no authority except that which God has established. The authorities that exist have been established by God" (Romans 13:1).

Goal

We seek through our study of Romans 13 to recognize the state as an institution established by God for our well-being by preserving a stable and peaceful civil order within which the church can go about its distinctive work of proclaiming the Gospel.

What's Going On Here?

Good citizenship is founded on the Christian belief that God orders, preserves, and enhances His creation through government. Romans 13 presents a key part of the New Testament's teaching on the Christian's relationship to the governing powers. God is the source of government's authority, and the institutions of government dare never overstep their divinely imposed boundaries. Christians are thankful for this evidence of God's care, and they will seize every opportunity to speak the Gospel in the peaceful and orderly setting that government affords.

Searching the Scriptures

1. Read Romans 13:1–7. Why does the Christian owe obedience and compliance to the government (vv. 1–2)? What are the two reasons for compliance given in verse 5?

2. The New Testament refers to the Christian's duties toward the civil government in a number of places outside of Romans 13. On the basis of 1 Timothy 2:1–3; Titus 3:1–2; and 1 Peter 2:13–17, list several of those duties. What is the reason given for Christian actions toward government? See also Titus 2:11–14.

3. What criterion will the Christian use in finally determining *in a particular instance* whether a dictate of the government is to be obeyed? See Acts 5:29.

4. Why is love the foundation of Christian behavior (Romans 13:10; see also 1 John 4:19–21)?

5. Romans 13:12 instructs us to "put on the armor of light." Read Ephesians 6:10–18 as well. What spiritual equipment makes up this armor?

The Word for Us

1. How might rulers abuse this chapter from Romans 13? Consider, among others, the example of King David (2 Samuel 11) and Nathan's words from God (2 Samuel 12:7–10).

2. Paul challenges Christians to "clothe yourselves with the Lord Jesus Christ" (Romans 13:14). What does being clothed with Christ mean to you? Galatians 3:27 may be helpful.

Closing

Gracious God, keep our nation under Your care. Bless the leaders of our land that we may be a people at peace among ourselves and a blessing to other nations of the earth. Help us provide trustworthy leaders, contribute to wise decisions for the general welfare, and thus serve You faithfully, to the honor of Your holy name; through Jesus Christ, our Lord. Amen.

Lesson 13

Living to the Lord
(Romans 14–16)

Theme Verses

"For none of us lives to himself alone and none of us dies to himself alone. If we live, we live to the Lord; and if we die, we die to the Lord. So, whether we live or die, we belong to the Lord" (Romans 14:7–8).

Goal

We seek to recognize that any status we may enjoy is ours exclusively as a gift from God through the work of Jesus Christ. Our desire is to serve and sacrifice for a weaker brother or sister, realizing that we have no privileged or superior claim to God's favor.

What's Going On Here?

Because we all stand before God as forgiven sinners, justified solely by His grace in Jesus Christ, the body of Christ has no room for attitudes of superiority or arrogance. When our freedom from the Law is not the issue, we will act in love to make personal sacrifices so that a brother or sister will not stumble and so that the unity of the church might be preserved. God's grace, not our displays of piety, is the source of our hope, joy, and abiding peace.

As Romans concludes, we can see that Paul's single concern is to encourage the proclamation of the unconditional Gospel of Jesus Christ to as wide an audience as possible. Moreover, the church as the people of God is the place where God is active in grace. Accordingly, Paul recognizes the valuable contributions made to his work by all of his brothers and sisters in the body of Christ.

Searching the Scriptures

1. Read Romans 14:5–6 and Colossians 2:16–17. What makes a dish of food or a certain day "holy"? See also 1 Timothy 4:4–5 and 1 Corinthians 10:31.

2. Paul uses the phrase "to the Lord" or "to God" eight times in Romans 14:5–8. What does it mean to eat, to live, or to die "to the Lord"?

3. On the basis of Romans 14:13–18 what is at stake in doing something another person believes is wrong, even if we are convinced that it is right (see especially v. 15)? What motivation will prevent us from distressing another Christian by what we do? What is the relationship between these matters and the kingdom of God?

4. Read Romans 15:14. What approach does Paul use in inspiring and leading his readers? See 1 Corinthians 1:4–7 for another example of Paul's leadership style.

5. Read Romans 15:25–28. What made the collection for the poor of Jerusalem so important for Paul? In what sense were the Gentiles in debt to the Jews?

6. In Romans 16:25–26 Paul recapitulates the essence of His Gospel. By way of review, what is the proclamation of the Gospel about? When was it revealed? For whom? To what end?

The Word for Us

1. Why are believers not frightened by the accounting spoken of in Romans 14:10b, 12? See also Ephesians 2:8–9 and 1 John 2:1–2.

2. Together, the endurance and encouragement provided through the Scriptures result in hope (Romans 15:4). Who is the focus of that hope for us today? See also 1 Timothy 4:10 and 6:17.

3. Read Romans 15:5–7. In the church at Rome, Jews and Gentiles came together as God's people. It was sometimes difficult to do what Paul asked them to do—to "accept one another." What motivation did Paul offer for such mutual acceptance (v. 7)? Also, what is the goal of preserving and promoting the church's spiritual unity (vv. 5–6; see also John 17:20–23)?

Closing

May we Your precepts, Lord, fulfill
And do on earth our Father's will
    As angels do above;
Still walk in Christ, the living way,
With all Your children and obey
    The law of Christian love.

So may we join Your name to bless,
Your grace adore, Your pow'r confess,
    To flee from sin and strife.
One is our calling, one our name,
The end of all our hopes the same,
    A glorious crown of life.

Spirit of life, of love and peace,
Our hearts unite, our joy increase,
    Your gracious help supply.
To each of us the blessing give
In Christian fellowship to live,
    In joyful hope to die.

ROMANS
Alive in Christ

Leaders Notes

Preparing to Teach Romans

In preparation to teach, consult an introduction to the book of Romans (such as the one in the *Concordia Self-Study Bible*) and the section on Romans in the *Concordia Self-Study Commentary*. Another excellent resource is *Romans: A Commentary* by Martin H. Franzmann (CPH).

Also read the text in a modern translation. The NIV is referred to in the lesson comments.

In the section "Searching the Scriptures," the leader serves as a guide using the questions given (or others) to help the class discover what the text actually says. This is a major part of teaching, namely, directing the learners to discover for themselves. Another major portion of each lesson is helping the students by discussion to see the meaning for our times, for church and world today, and especially for our own lives.

Group Bible Study

Group Bible study means mutual learning from one another under the guidance of a leader or facilitator. The Bible is an inexhaustible resource. No one person can discover all it has to offer. In a class many eyes see many things and can apply them to many life situations. The leader should resist the temptation to "give the answers" and so act as an "authority." This teaching approach stifles participation by individual members and can actually hamper learning. As a general rule the teacher is not to "give interpretation" but to "develop interpreters." Of course there are times when the leader should and must share insights and information gained by his or her own deeper research. The ideal class is one in which the leader guides class members through the lesson and engages them in meaningful sharing and discussion at all points, leading them to a summary of the lesson at the close. As a general rule, don't tell the participants what they can discover by themselves.

The general aim of every Bible study is to help people grow spiritually, not merely in biblical and theological knowledge, but also in Christian thinking and living. This means growth in Christian attitudes, insights, and skills for Christian living. The focus of this course must be the church and the world of our day. The guiding question will be, What does the Lord teach us for life today through the book of Romans?

Pace Your Teaching

Do not try to cover every question in each lesson. This attempt would lead to undue haste and frustration. Be selective. Pace your teaching. Spend no more than five minutes with "Theme Verses" and "Goal" and two or three minutes with "What's Going On Here?" Allow 20 minutes to apply the lesson ("The Word for Us") and five minutes for "Closing." This schedule, you will notice, allows only about 30 minutes for working with the text ("Searching the Scriptures").

Should your group have more than a one-hour class period, you can take it more leisurely. But do not allow any lesson to "drag" and become tiresome. Keep it moving. Keep it alive. Keep it deeply meaningful. Eliminate some questions and restrict yourself to those questions most meaningful to the members of the class. If most members study the text at home, they can report their findings, and the time gained can be applied to relating the lesson to life.

Good Preparation

Good preparation by the leader usually affects the pleasure and satisfaction the class will experience.

Suggestions to the Leader for Using the Study Guide

The Lesson Pattern

The material in this guide is designed to aid *Bible study*, that is, a consideration of the written Word of God, with discussion and personal application growing out of the text at hand. The typical lesson is divided into these sections:

1. "Theme Verses"
2. "Goal"
3. "What's Going On Here?"
4. "Searching the Scriptures"
5. "The Word for Us"
6. "Closing"

"Theme Verses" and "Goal" give the leader assistance in arousing the interest of the group in the concepts of the lesson. Do not linger too long over the introductory remarks. You merely show that the material to be studied is meaningful to Christian faith and life today.

"What's Going On Here?" helps you gain an understanding of the textual portion to be considered in the session. Before the text is broken down for closer scrutiny, it should be seen in the perspective of a greater whole. At this point the class leader takes the participants to a higher elevation to show them the general layout of the lesson. The overview gives the group an idea where it is going, what individual places are to be visited, and how the two are interrelated.

"Searching the Scriptures" provides the real "spadework" necessary for Bible study. Here the class digs, uncovers, and discovers; it gets the facts and observes them. Comment from the leader is needed only to the extent that it helps the group understand the text. The questions in the study guide are intended to help the learners discover the meaning of the text.

Having determined what the text says, the class is ready to apply the message. Having heard, read, marked, and learned the Word of God, we proceed to digest it inwardly through discussion, evaluation, and application. This is done, as the study guide suggests, by taking the truths of Romans and applying them to the world and Christianity in general and then to personal Christian life. Class time may not permit discussion of all questions and topics.

Remember, the Word of God is sacred, but the study guide is not. The guide offers only suggestions. The leader should not hesitate to alter the guidelines or substitute others to meet his or her needs and the needs of the participants. Adapt your teaching plan to your class and your class period. Good teaching directs the learner to discover for himself or herself. For the teacher this means directing the learner, not giving the learner answers. Choose the verses that should be looked up in Scripture. What discussion questions will you ask? At what points? Write them in the margin of your study guide. Involve class members, but give them clear directions.

Begin the class with prayer, and allow time for a brief time of worship at the end of the class session. Suggestions for closing devotions are given in the study guide. Remember to pray frequently outside of class for yourself and your class. May God the Holy Spirit bless your study and your leading of others into the comforting truths of God's Christ-centered Word.

Lesson 1
The Power of the Gospel

The Class Session
Have volunteers read "Theme Verses," "Goal," and "What's Going On Here?"

Searching the Scriptures
1. Despite our best efforts to conceal it, human godlessness and wickedness have been exposed and are subject to the wrath of God.

2. The essential character of idolatry is to put anyone or anything other than God first in our lives. We look to that someone or something else as the source of our personal identity, the basis for meaning in our lives, and the source of our eternal security. In this section of Romans, this is captured in 1:25: "they exchanged the truth of God for a lie, *and worshiped and served created things rather than the Creator.*" The other verses in this shorter section are largely commentary on this text.

3. Finally, when we are persistent and obstinate in our idolatry, God will "give us over" (1:24, 26, 28) to the consequences of this idolatry.

4. The sins enumerated in Romans 1:22–32 are a consequence of our broken relationship with God. What's more, they in turn have a cumulative and enslaving effect, so that sin traps us in a vicious and inescapable circle: "Although they know God's righteous decree that those who do such things deserve death, they not only continue to do these very things but also approve of those who practice them."

5. In these verses and consistently in St. Paul's letters, the righteousness of God refers to the gift that God gives to men and women through the Gospel of Jesus Christ. Indeed, that is the crucial point of the theme verses in 1:16–17: "For in the Gospel [literally, in Greek, "in it," pointing back to the Gospel of verse 16] a righteousness of God is revealed. ..."

6. In 1:17, St. Paul quotes the Old Testament prophet Habakkuk to affirm that human beings have the righteousness of God through faith—which is itself a consequence of our hearing the Gospel, through which the Holy Spirit works (look ahead to Romans 10, especially vv. 14–17).

7. Paul's confidence always was anchored in the power of the Gospel itself, which in fact carried with it the very power of God. The word *power* in 1:16 is "dynamic": the Gospel has the power to accomplish its purpose, namely, to announce forgiveness and to engender faith in Jesus Christ.

The Word for Us

1. Though he was best known as the apostle to the Gentiles, Paul's gospel was for all people, whatever their religious background. This affirmation is rooted in the fact that all human beings relate to God on the basis of Jesus Christ, who is the Savior of all people. Naturally, this means that our outreach should be as universal as the apostle's. Just as no one is without sin, it is even more important to emphasize that the Gospel of Jesus Christ is for everyone.

2. As the comments about idolatry serve to indicate, the relationship with God is always primary. While our idolatry destroys that relationship, God restores it through the Gospel. When the relationship to God is healthy, we will avoid the kinds of sins Paul describes in Romans 1. Looking back to the theme verses, we see that because the righteousness of God is God's gift in the Gospel that is ours through faith, we are comforted with the knowledge that this righteousness is not something we have to attain through our own flawed and futile efforts.

3. God's Law has several uses, but the most important of these is to give us a clear and honest picture of ourselves, much like a mirror. That "mirror" exposes our sin; and when we see that sin, we also realize the need for rescue. The Law won't and can't provide the means of this rescue. That's where the Gospel comes in. While New Testament letters were not written to be outlined in neat convenient patterns, Paul nonetheless consistently uses the Gospel as God's answer to the futility exposed by the Law.

Closing

Follow the suggestion in the study guide.

Lesson 2

Righteousness Apart from Law

The Class Session

Have volunteers read "Theme Verses," "Goal," and "What's Going On Here?"

Searching the Scriptures

1. The warning in 2:1 is especially pertinent for certain groups among

the Jews, most notably the Pharisees, who were zealous about adhering to the details of the Law, while being themselves guilty of some of the same sins Paul condemns in Romans 1. Some first-century Jews looked down on Gentiles because of their ignorance of the Old Testament Law and because they led outwardly immoral lives.

2. Kindness, tolerance, and patience have characterized God's way of dealing with human beings from the beginning. The goal is stated in the last part of 2:4: "God's kindness leads you toward repentance." Some Jews had mistakenly believed that God's forbearance meant that He did not intend to judge at all.

3. The New Testament in general and these texts from Romans in particular make it clear that all human beings are saved by God's gift of righteousness in Jesus Christ (1:16). The conduct that is praised in these verses and that will be rewarded at the coming judgment is possible only through faith in Jesus Christ (see John 15:5; Hebrews 11:6). Conversely, the conduct described here that invites judgment arises out of a broken relationship with God. No one has a privileged position, nor is anyone able to relate to God apart from Jesus Christ (see also John 14:6; Acts 4:12; 1 Timothy 2:5–6).

4. Romans 2:15 gives Paul's answer: "They show that the requirements of the law are written on their hearts." The apostle does not mean that Gentiles adhered to the precepts of the Old Testament Law, but that all human beings are created so that, in their hearts, they know the kinds of things God's Law (namely, the Decalog or Ten Commandments) requires. As Paul notes in connection with the Gentiles, both their actions and their conscience make that clear.

5. This section is a vivid contrast between hypocrisy and faithfulness, between empty pretense and consecrated practice. One's identity as a child of God is marked by fidelity and its corresponding lifestyle, not by external sins in themselves. "Circumcision" was one of the most important signs by which God's people were to be identified (see Genesis 17:10–11; Leviticus 12:3). But it had been perverted to mean a guarantee of God's goodwill regardless of the conduct of His people. In this way, it was emptied of its meaning. The inner circumcision of the heart, performed by God's Spirit, is more meaningful than an external, physical act (see also Deuteronomy 30:6).

6. Paul has consistently sought to show that whatever their differences (e.g., the Jews have been given the Law, circumcision, etc.), both Jews and Gentiles have brought upon themselves God's indictment for their sin. "Jews and Gentiles alike are all under sin" (v. 9). "There is no one righteous, not even one" (v. 10).

7. As Paul notes at the end of verse 19, the law holds all human beings accountable. There is no escape. Verse 20 points to the most important function of the Law, one which will be even clearer in the context of the remainder of chapter 3: God's Law *always* exposes human sin.

God's Word for Us

1. In ways similar to those described by Jesus in the Sermon on the Mount, we may not be guilty of publicly disreputable acts. Often, however, at the level of intention or disposition we are guilty of some of the same kinds of sins.

2. The Law in itself is a wonderful gift from God; how we sometimes make use of the Law is the problem. These chapters should disabuse us of any and all self-righteousness, and, most importantly, of any overt or subtle attempts to justify ourselves on the basis of the Law.

Closing

Follow the suggestion in the study guide.

Lesson 3

"Righteousness from God"

The Class Session

Have volunteers read "Theme Verses," "Goal," and "What's Going On Here?"

Searching the Scriptures

1. To be sure, human attainment of the righteousness of God, if this means the righteousness that God is and has in Himself, is impossible. It is a cause for fear and even despair. But Romans 3:21–22 makes it clear that the righteousness discussed here is not something that God demands from us, but something that He gives freely through the Gospel. This is a righteousness *from* God, which comes through faith in Jesus Christ. St. Paul makes the same point in Philippians 3:9: "… not having a righteousness of my own that comes from the law, but that which is through faith in Christ—the righteousness that comes from God and is by faith."

2. That is precisely Paul's point: Nothing! Works of law are not the way

to enter God's favor. The Gospel announces that God is favorable to us already in Jesus Christ. So there is nothing left for us to do. "This righteousness from God comes *through faith in Jesus Christ* to all who believe" (v. 22). Through faith we focus not on ourselves but on the God who gives freely, without conditions. God says, in effect, "Stop trying to *do;* instead, *trust,* for I have already taken care of everything.

3. Certainly, believing is a work, and a good one at that. But believing is not a work of the Law by which we seek to win God's approval. In fact, we believe only because God's Spirit has been at work in us through the Gospel—on our own and left to our own natural powers we are "dead in transgressions" and are incapable of generating our own faith. The key verses here are Romans 3:28, "we maintain that a man is justified by faith apart from observing the law"; and Ephesians 2:8, "it is by grace you have been saved, through faith—and this is not from yourselves, it is the gift of God—not by works, so that no one can boast."

4. No one is able to approach God on the basis of his or her own accomplishments, for all have sinned and all fall short of the glory of God. Likewise, these same sinners are received into God's favor in the same way: through the work of Jesus Christ for us. This is the only way; and for this we should be grateful, because no other way would be adequate. See also 3:29–30.

5. They are the free gifts of God's grace—His undeserved mercy— and they are both rooted in and inseparable from the work of Jesus Christ.

6. Justification comes through Jesus Christ as He takes our place under the accusation and indictment of the law and suffers its penalty—judgment—for us. See Romans 4:25; 2 Corinthians 5:21; and Galatians 3:13.

Likewise, the price of our redemption from our slavery to sin is the blood of Jesus Christ (see 1 John 1:7; and especially Ephesians 1:7, "In Him we have redemption through His blood, the forgiveness of sins, in accordance with the riches of God's grace").

7. "Sacrifice of atonement" is a more idiomatic way of translating a Greek word that is often rendered "propitiation" or "expiation." When the New Testament asserts that Jesus is a sacrifice of atonement or is the propitiation for our sins, it is using a concept from Old Testament worship and sacrifice, which refers to the mercy seat of the ark of the covenant. The high priest on the Day of Atonement sprinkled the blood of sacrificial animals on this lid, or cover. In the light of the New Testament fulfillment in Jesus Christ, this language proclaims to the people that God does not look upon their sins, for these have been covered by the sacrificial blood of the Lamb of God (see also John 1:29). By the action of God on the cross the guilt of sin is taken away, and the righteousness and mercy of God are

manifested.

In view of and for the sake of the sacrifice of Christ, God received Old Testament believers and declared them righteous. Today God receives us sinners and bestows on us the righteousness of Christ won for us by His atoning death on the cross.

The Word for Us

1. The God who justifies us is the God of all humanity. Therefore, Jesus Christ is the only way of salvation. To people caught up in their own efforts to please God—on the assumption that their work is a prerequisite to enjoying His favor—we have the opportunity of declaring the mercy of the one God who provides salvation for all people (circumcised and uncircumcised alike) in Jesus Christ. Rather than having the burden of convincing others that their religion or theology is wrong, we can rely on the comfort and persuasive power of the Gospel itself.

2. Paul's critics argued that he was introducing something new, thus abolishing the entire heritage of Israel. But Paul maintained (as we will see at length in Romans 4) that the entire Old Testament witnessed to the righteousness that the gracious God would provide through the Messiah. Moreover, the Gospel announces what some people were trying to achieve by the Law—life with God. The person who understands the Gospel also sees the Law in its true light. It is the mirror that reveals to us our inability to ascend to God through our own efforts and our need for the righteousness that God bestows as a free gift through faith in Jesus Christ.

Closing

Follow the suggestion in the study guide.

Lesson 4

Promise and Faith

The Class Session

Have volunteers read "Theme Verses," "Goal," and "What's Going On Here?"

Searching the Scriptures

1. God's relationship with us is not based on a contract or about the performance of required duties. Instead, it is based on God's Gospel promise to give us the righteousness of Jesus Christ. "Faith is credited as righteousness" (v. 5).

Note especially the reference to "the wicked" in verse 5. Not only are human beings not quite good enough, they are "ungodly," as most English translations render the word. This term sharpens the point Paul is making: Justification is a pure gift (see Romans 3:24) to those who are under the wrath of God (see Romans 1:18).

In this same connection note also the last theme verse, 4:17b—"God … gives life to the dead and calls things that are not as though they were."

2. Abraham's circumcision came after God made His promise to Him, and after Abraham had heard the promise in faith. For this reason, Abraham can also be called the "father of all who believe," which extends to uncircumcised Gentiles as well as to circumcised Jews. The promise and faith are primary; circumcision is an outward sign.

3. The Gospel announces that God is merciful to all people for the sake of Jesus Christ. Men and women are saved by grace through faith, just as Abraham was. Ethnicity is never the issue. Because the promise comes by grace through faith (v. 16), it is never based on the possession of the written Law.

4. It is clear from both chapters 3 and 4 that justification is not about personal performance or our attainment of righteousness. Justification is about God giving to us something that we cannot earn: The righteousness of Jesus Christ, which is given to us in the Gospel (Romans 1:16–17) and received through faith (Romans 3:21–31).

5. The Christian recognizes that Jesus' death is a consequence of his or her own sinful and hopeless situation. At the same time, the resurrection is God's acceptance of the perfect sacrifice of Jesus for us. Because of the resurrection, we know that death is not the last word, and we know that God keeps His promises. The resurrection makes our hope certain and assures us of everlasting life.

The Word for Us

1. To live by the Law is to live by one's own achievement. Not only is it obvious that our achievement falls short, the larger point is that this is not how God relates to us. Our God is a God who gives freely and abundantly, not one who dispenses wages or rewards for a service rendered. The appropriate response to a promise is trust and confidence; faith rejoices in the gifts God gives and not in the rules that are obeyed.

Living by faith and living by Law are mutually exclusive because they are two entirely different ways of relating to God. Living under the Law seeks to relate to God on the basis of what we do; living by faith relates to God on the basis of what He has done for us in Jesus Christ.

2. First, and most basically, we are justified by God's grace in Jesus Christ, and never by our works or accomplishments. Second, and in connection with Romans 4, not even Abraham, one of the great "heroes" of the Bible, was chosen by God on the basis of his works but on the basis of God's promise. When Abraham is praised (here in Romans 4 and in Hebrews 11:8–12, 17–19) he is praised for his faith in the promise—in the face of every empirical reason to doubt it—and never for a blameless life.

Closing

Follow the suggestion in the study guide.

Lesson 5

Adam versus Christ

The Class Session

Have volunteers read "Theme Verses," "Goal," and "What's Going On Here?"

Searching the Scriptures

1. This peace is not just a situation of "no-conflict" or an absence of hostility. "Peace" here in Romans and in the Bible generally is about a relationship that God brings about with His people. It means that all is now right between God and His creatures, specifically because of the reconciliation accomplished by Jesus Christ and His intercession on our behalf.

It is also important to note that "peace" here is not about one's feelings, which can come and go. It is an objective fact—there is now peace between God and His human creatures—based on the death and resurrection of Jesus Christ.

2. Hope in these verses is not optimism or positive thinking. It is certain because it is based on the completed work of Jesus at the cross, of which the Holy Spirit perpetually reminds us.

3. Verse 6a notes that human beings are "powerless," and thus cannot contribute to their own salvation. Verse 6b repeats Paul's statement from Romans 4:5 that Christ died for the "ungodly." Verse 8 notes that Christ died for us "while we were still sinners." Verse 10 may be the most emphatic statement in this regard anywhere in the New Testament: "when we were God's enemies, we were reconciled to Him through the death of His Son." Human beings on their own and apart from a faith-relationship with God are not ambivalent or neutral, they are only helpless. The natural man or woman is an enemy of God, actively hostile to and in rebellion against Him; and it is this hostility that is removed by the sacrificial death of Christ for us and in our place.

4. One of the crucial points Paul makes in this letter is that justification, redemption, and reconciliation are not things that can or might happen. Instead, they have been accomplished through the death and resurrection of Jesus. There is nothing outstanding that is left to be done.

5. Adam's sin introduced sin to the world, and with it judgment, condemnation, and death for all people. Jesus' death and resurrection manifested and extended God's grace, Christ's righteousness, justification, and life (all of which are interrelated terms) to all people. Salvation is available for all through faith (Romans 5:1–2).

6. When Paul observed that "where sin increased, grace increased all the more," he is not saying that God somehow matches human sin with His grace. Rather, God's grace triumphs over human sin. Not even human sin is able to thwart His plan of salvation and get in the way of the gifts God seeks to give us in Jesus Christ.

The Word for Us

1. Our confidence is as strong as the God who has accomplished our justification, redemption, and reconciliation. It is never a matter of how devout we are—or even of how strong our faith is. Whatever the ups and downs of our lives might be, they cannot undermine the accomplished reality of the death and resurrection of Jesus. Faith justifies not because of how strong it may be—sometimes it might not be very strong at all—but because it trusts the Gospel promise that God has kept in Jesus.

2. Paul realized that the Gospel did not mean that all of one's problems

would disappear. Indeed, living the Christian life may bring its own set of problems. Paul had his share of problems. The Gospel does not remove the problems, but gives us a lens through which we can understand their place in their lives. The sufferings produce perseverance, character, and hope. They are part of the human condition—a sinful human condition whose consequences were borne by Jesus Christ on the cross for us and in our stead. The pain that may attend these problems is never the only or final word. The Word that must be heard in the midst of these moments is the Word of God's presence with us in Jesus Christ and the Word of forgiveness He declares to us.

Closing

Follow the suggestion in the study guide.

Lesson 6

Baptism, Death, and Resurrection

The Class Session

Have volunteers read "Theme Verses," "Goal," and "What's Going On Here?"

Searching the Scriptures

1. The basis is the accomplished fact of what has happened in Baptism. "We died [past tense] to sin" (v. 2). We have been baptized into the death and resurrection of Jesus Christ. Paul elaborates on the consequences of this Baptism in verses 5–7: "… Our old self was crucified with Him so that the body of sin might be done away with, that we should no longer be slaves to sin—*because anyone who has died has been freed from sin.*" Something that has died can no longer dominate or determine our existence.

2. By linking what takes place in Baptism to the death and resurrection of Christ (see also Colossians 2:12), our resurrection can be understood as an event that is already experienced in the present. At the same time, our resurrection is also something in the future, to which we can look forward with certain hope because this hope is anchored in the accomplished reality of the empty tomb of Jesus.

3. Verses 11 and 14b state the accomplished reality: We are dead to sin but alive to God in Christ Jesus (v. 11), and we are not under the law, but under grace (v. 14). These realities are the starting points of our Christian life. Given these realities, we will not let sin reign, nor devote our bodies to wickedness. Rather, we will offer ourselves and our bodies to God for service to Him and as "instruments of righteousness."

4. The obedience that Christians render to God is not something that can be coerced or extracted from them. Enforced compliance is legalism. The essence of the Christian life is willing service, and it is performed not for a master who demands but for a merciful God who has forgiven us, freed us from our slavery to sin, and who promises an eternal future with Him.

5. "Wages" are earned or merited as remuneration for a task or obligation performed. The remuneration is something we deserve. "Gift," on the other hand, is something for which we can make no claim, but comes to us entirely out of the generosity of the giver. The sin that enslaves human beings leads to a well-deserved fate: death. This is Law. But the point of the Gospel is that God does not give us what we deserve. He gives not on the basis of what we do but on the basis of His grace expressed in Jesus Christ. When He gives from this source, we receive eternal life through Him who gave His life into death for us.

The Word for Us

1. Paul consistently denies that God's free grace and forgiveness make it immaterial whether we sin or not. Because we have died to sin in Baptism, we cannot and will not give free reign to sin. To do so is a spiritually impossible. To be sure, we do follow God's guidelines in the Ten Commandments, and in the various places where the same things are discussed in the New Testament. The key point is that people of God through faith in Jesus, follow the commandments not because they have to or need to in order to earn God's favor; we follow them out of a sense of thanksgiving. As one saying describes it, with admittedly less than perfect grammar, "It's not something we got to do; it's something we get to do."

2. The use of the singular rather than the plural underscores the fact that human sin is not only about individual actions that we do or should not do. Sin is nearly personified by Paul. It is a force with which we must contend and one that seeks to enslave us. It will not give us up voluntarily; instead, it has to be conquered and we have to be freed from its domination. The issue, then, is not merely about those things we do, but about who or what our master is. This helps explain why the First Commandment is the most important one, and the one that determines our faithfulness to the other nine.

3. However much he may have been assailed by spiritual affliction or anxiety, Luther could point to *God's* action in Baptism, through which God claimed him as His own. Baptism meant that in the face of the Law's accusation, he could claim the Gospel's definitive expression of forgiveness. Baptism for Luther meant that death and resurrection was his experience as well as that of his Lord. "[Baptism] works forgiveness of sins, delivers from death and the devil, and gives eternal salvation to all who believe this, as the words and promises of God declare." (Small Catechism, IV)

Closing

Follow the suggestion in the study guide.

Lesson 7

The Struggle Within

The Class Session

Have volunteers read "Theme Verses," "Goal," and "What's Going On Here?"

Searching the Scriptures

1. In both of these texts, Paul talks about our dying, specifically, our dying to sin (see 6:2, 6–7). This dying takes place in the washing of Baptism. But so too does resurrection, and as a consequence of our death and resurrection we are released from the condemnation of the Law (7:6). The Christian life is empowered by the Gospel and is energized by the Spirit ("the new way of the Spirit"). It is not motivated by the Law.

2. The Law is holy, righteous, and good (vv. 12–13), and it was intended to bring life (v. 10). But when this Law acts on a sinful nature that is hostile to God, it exposes sin (v. 7) and even awakens and arouses further sin (vv. 8–9). Obstinate, rebellious people sometimes do things precisely because they are forbidden. When directed to and against sinful people, the Law brings death (vv. 11, 13).

3. To be a slave is to be the captive possession of someone or something, and to have no freedom. Slavery to sin and what it entails is explained in verses 15–24.

4. "Law" here seems to mean some other principle or force at work. In

Romans 7 Paul personifies the Law as tempter (v. 11) or as a stern taskmaster (v. 14).

5. These verses highlight the utter futility of human existence under the power of sin and the indictment of the Law (v. 24). The transitional paragraph is given in verse 24b—"Who will rescue me from this body of death?" The answer, which calls for immediate thanksgiving, is Jesus Christ.

The Word for Us

1. As most study Bibles and commentaries acknowledge, one can argue either way. However, the balance of evidence seems to indicate that Paul is describing the situation that a person is in even after his or her conversion, where there is a perpetual struggle between the renewed will, which desires to follow God's law, and one's sinful nature (Greek: one's "flesh," though as the NIV's translation indicates, not to be understood in a physical sense), which always needs to be subdued.

2. Human beings were not only rescued from sin and death; rather, these forces have themselves been put to death through Baptism (7:4, 6). "[We] belong to another, to Him who was raised from the dead, in order that we might bear fruit to God" (7:4). "We have been released from the law so that we serve in the new way of the Spirit, and not in the old way of the written code" (7:6). Finally, even when we fall, forgiveness and rescue are ours in Jesus Christ (7:24–25). Thus, sin and the Law can never have the last word. See also 1 Corinthians 10:13 for another of God's promises in the midst of struggle and temptation.

3. It may well be more intense for a Christian. The Christian is more acutely aware of how powerful a force sin can be and is in his or her life. More specifically, the Christian is able to see it for what it is and is aware of the consequences of the battle. Christians recognize that even with all we have been given, we still are tempted and often fall. Also, the Christian knows what is at stake in these struggles.

Closing

Follow the suggestion in the study guide.

Lesson 8

No Condemnation

The Class Session

Have volunteers read "Theme Verses," "Goal," and "What's Going On Here?"

Searching the Scriptures

1. In the wake of all that has gone before—where Paul has used language such as "waging war" (7:23), "prisoner" (7:23b), and "slave" (7:25b)—that no matter how intense the struggle might be, the law cannot condemn those who are in Jesus Christ. When the Law makes its accusation heard, the Holy Spirit communicates to us the life won for us by the coming of Jesus Christ into the flesh (Romans 8:2–5). The Spirit is the controlling force in our lives, not the law and sin and death (vv. 5–17).

2. Jesus is not a distant or detached savior, but He is one who became a true human being (i.e., the incarnation, or the Son of God becoming flesh in the person of Jesus) in every respect. Unlike all other human beings, however, He was sinless, so that He did not have to suffer and die for His own sins.

3. Our lives and our bodies are not our own; they now belong to God and our bodies are the dwelling place of the Holy Spirit. God has bought us (i.e., redeemed) back from sin, and our loyalty is now to Him and not to our old masters. Jesus' resurrection and the Holy Spirit living within us is the assurance of our own resurrection. In fact, the Holy Spirit represents the "down payment," making certain our future inheritance and our resurrection of the dead. See also Ephesians 1:13–14; 2 Corinthians 1:22; and Romans 5:5.

4. We are predestined to be conformed to the image of God's Son; and God does this by calling us by the Gospel, justifying us, and finally glorifying us. Most important of all in any consideration of eternal election is that God does all of these things not arbitrarily but always *in Jesus Christ*. See especially Ephesians 1:4–5.

5. Jesus Christ died on our behalf. He was resurrected for us. And now He is interceding for us. With all of this going for us, Paul can ask the rhetorical question in verse 35: "Who shall separate us from the love of Christ? Shall trouble or hardship or persecution or famine or nakedness or danger or sword?" Note: This may be a list of hardships that Paul and his party experienced at the hands of those who were hostile to the Gospel.

The Word for Us

1. We know that Jesus has experienced everything we have, including all kinds of temptation (see Matthew 4:1–11). He has not only "related to us" in the most intense and profound way—He literally became one of us. And what He did in His life, His death on the cross, and at His empty tomb was done entirely for us. He entered into our struggles and conquered sin, death, and the devil. Now the sinless and victorious Savior remains incessantly active on our behalf. "Christ Jesus, who died—more than that, who was raised to life—is at the right hand of God and is also interceding for us" (Romans 8:34).

2. Our obligation is not to live according to the sinful nature. Positively, this means living for the One who redeemed us. As we live for Him we communicate the Gospel of redemption to others. Such obligations are not the duties of Law, but the privileges of one who has heard the call of the Gospel.

3. The Holy Spirit, who through the Gospel reminds us of our adoption as God's sons and daughters, is the antidote to fear. When we cry, "Abba, Father" by the power of the Spirit, we are using the same expression of intimacy that Jesus used in conversing with the Father. See Mark 14:36, Jesus' prayer in the Garden of Gethsemane. The closeness Jesus enjoyed with His own Father is now reflected in our own filial relationship with God. See also Romans 8:26–27.

4. Of the many Gospel truths that the doctrine of election communicates, two of the most significant are that, first, God has planned our salvation from eternity, so that His accomplishment of our redemption was not an afterthought; and, second, God has taken care of literally everything for our salvation. There is nothing outstanding that still needs to be done.

Closing

Follow the suggestion in the study guide.

Lesson 9

Jesus Christ—The End of the Law

The Class Session

Have volunteers read "Theme Verses," "Goal," and "What's Going On Here?"

Searching the Scriptures

1. Israelites have enjoyed a status as God's adopted children; they have experienced the divine glory (glory often understood in the Old Testament as the presence of God); they have been the recipients of the covenants (to Abraham in Genesis 15; to the whole people in Exodus 24; to David in 2 Samuel 23; and the "new covenant" of Jeremiah 31) that God made with them at various times, which in their character are unilateral acts of grace; they have received the Law, climactically at Sinai; their temple was the dwelling place of God, where the sacrifices took place; they were the recipients of numerous promises of a coming Redeemer; and, finally, from the line of patriarchs beginning with Abraham has come *the* promised Redeemer, Jesus Christ.

2. If God acted on the strict basis of justice, no one would or could be saved. The Law exposes the sin of all people. The issue is not so much "why this one?" or "why not those?" Rather, the issue is why anyone at all. To that more fundamental question the answer is always and only God's grace.

3. God shows extraordinary patience even to these who would eventually be objects of His wrath. The purpose of this patience is to effect repentance. Regarding the Hosea passages, while in the eighth century before Christ they may have pointed to the spiritual restoration of Israel, in Romans 9 they are applied to the Gentiles, to whom God would extend His promise and make them part of the "new Israel." The Isaiah text illustrates the point made in verse 27 that a small remnant of Israel would be saved.

4. Israel attempted to secure their relationship with God by their obedience to the Law. Two problems always follow this approach. First, our sin makes such obedience impossible; and, most importantly, God seeks to relate to us on the basis of His promise and faith, not on the basis of works of Law.

5. Gentiles obtained God's righteousness purely and exclusively by grace, that is, the undeserved mercy of God proclaimed in Jesus Christ.

6. Christ puts an end to the condemnation of the Law and decisively closes off the route of the Law as a way of relating to God or obtaining righteousness. One cannot gain the righteousness of God by means of the Law. Instead, our righteousness comes solely from God in Christ and from no other source. The burden of somehow aspiring to God's righteousness by our own Law-driven achievements is lifted. Christ has fulfilled the Law.

7. God has made unnecessary the extraordinary works depicted here. They are unnecessary because the risen Jesus is Lord (v. 9), and salvation is already present for those who believe.

The Word for Us

1. To state it very simply, as one who knew how the mercy of God could

overcome resistance in his own life, Paul never gives up. From the book of Acts, one can read that the first place Paul went when he arrived in a new city was the synagog, where Jews and proselytes (i.e., usually those who had not taken the final step of circumcision on the way to becoming a Jew) naturally gathered. Also, if we look back to Romans 9:1–3, his "sorrow and unceasing anguish" is so intense that he could actually wish his own condemnation if it would mean the salvation of his people.

2. Not only is there no longer Jew or Gentile (Greek, Galatians 3:28), neither is there any longer slave nor free or male or female when it comes to our relationship with God. Before God we are all in the same position and share the same status: We are sinners in and of ourselves, all of us deserving judgment; and we are righteous only in Jesus Christ, with no one able to claim some privileged position. The appropriate model for the church, then, is not one based on privilege, hierarchy, or rank; instead, the appropriate question is how can we best serve one another in the context of a community formed by the Holy Spirit working through the Gospel.

3. God gives faith through the message of Jesus Christ. In fact, the Gospel is the means through which the Holy Spirit creates and sustains faith. Humanly speaking, there is no way for people to hear the Gospel if we don't communicate it to them in some way, whether by preaching, teaching, in writing, or personal sharing in some form.

Closing

Follow the suggestion in the study guide.

Lesson 10

The Remnant and "All Israel"

The Class Session

Have volunteers read "Theme Verses," "Goal," and "What's Going On Here?"

Searching the Scriptures

1. As in the time of Elijah, there is still a remnant who has embraced the message of the crucified and resurrected Jesus. From that remnant there can be, in the mercy and providence of God, a new outreach that extends

both to Jews and to Gentiles, from whom God creates a new people within which ethnic boundaries are broken down.

2. The remnant within Israel during the time of Paul refers to those who had responded in faith to the apostolic preaching that God had raised the crucified Jesus from the dead. The Jews had reasoned that since Jesus had been crucified, He could not be the Son of God or Messiah (Deuteronomy 21:23; Galatians 3:13). But the resurrection had changed all of that, as Peter put it in his Pentecost sermon: "Therefore let all Israel be assured of this: God has made this Jesus, whom you crucified, both Lord and Christ" (Acts 2:36). In this context, note especially the salutation of Romans (1:4–5) regarding Jesus: " … declared with power to be the Son of God by His resurrection from the dead: Jesus Christ our Lord." The confession that Jesus is Lord would characterize the remnant in Paul's (or anyone else's) time.

3. Paul characteristically holds out hope for their eventual conversion ("their fullness" in v. 12). In the wisdom of God's plan, sometimes hard to understand for human beings, some Jews will be won over as a consequence of Paul's work among the Gentiles.

4. The cultivated olive tree is the nation of Israel, whom God had called out of Egypt, planted in the land of Israel, and cultivated through the prophetic word. The wild olive shoot grafted in denotes Gentile Christians, who by faith are counted among God's people.

5. "All Israel" is not an ethnic or national designation. "Israel" in the New Testament is a theological term for the believing people of God. The same terms and designations that are applied to the nation of Israel in the Old Testament are applied to the church in the New Testament. See especially 1 Peter 2:9–10. Check the cross-references. So, all Israel in the context of these chapters refers to those who have responded in faith to the Gospel, a remnant from "old" Israel together with believing Gentiles.

God's Word for Us

1. As difficult as it may sometimes be to remember, it is God the Holy Spirit who works through the Gospel—indeed, who promises to work through it (see Isaiah 55:11). God is in control, not us. When our best efforts are rebuffed, we might follow Paul's model: Be patient, be loving, and be persistent.

2. Above all, Paul emphasizes that God creates a people for Himself based on grace alone in Jesus Christ. Everything we are and have, both present and eternal, comes as a result of the sovereign outpouring of His grace. This leads to a lifestyle characterized by confidence in His good and gracious will, freedom for service to others, and praise and thanksgiving.

Closing

Follow the suggestion in the study guide.

Lesson 11

Living Sacrifices

The Class Session

Have volunteers read "Theme Verses," "Goal," and "What's Going On Here?"

Searching the Scriptures

1. We "offer [our] bodies as living sacrifices" because of the mercy (Romans 12:1) and love (1 John 4:19) of God shown to us in Jesus Christ, who has made the one and only sacrifice necessary to pay for human sin. Our sacrifices are now pleasing to God because we are pleasing to God through faith in Jesus.

2. In verses 4–8, Paul likens the Christian community to the human body. Every part of the body has its own complementary role to play in its harmonious functioning. Similarly, all people have certain gifts that together contribute to the health and vitality of the body of believers, of which Jesus Christ Himself is the head. Not only do we all contribute to the strength and smooth working of the body of Christ, we also cannot function effectively as a body without each other—any more than our physical bodies can function at optimum efficiency with one of its members or organs missing.

3. Hope is ours on the basis of Jesus' resurrection from the dead, and such hope sustains us and enables us to be patient in times of affliction. Prayer is the means God gives to human beings to call for His help and strength. God answers our prayers and in affliction assures us that nothing can separate us from the love of God in Christ Jesus our Lord (Romans 8:39). Indeed, the same Jesus who died and was raised to life is now at the right hand of God interceding for us (Romans 8:34)

4. The two conditions are "if it is possible" and "as far as it depends on you." Paul was a realist; concord was not always possible. At the same time, division and discord should never be about superficial matters, or about matters of mere personal preference. With respect to the Romans,

Paul had not yet visited this congregation. But where he had worked, and where there had been conflict (e.g., Galatia, Corinth), the nonnegotiable issue always had to do with "the truth of the gospel" (Galatians 2:14). The truth of the Gospel could never be compromised. Short of that, Paul would counsel us to do everything in our power to get along.

5. By responding to a disagreeable person or to a person who has done us some injustice with kindness, instead of with anger or revenge, one may ultimately bring about his or her repentance. The quote from Proverbs 25:22, with its uncertain background in the ancient Near East, is admittedly difficult. It would seem to mean that in returning good for evil and by being kind to one's enemy, that enemy may repent or change.

The Word for Us

1. God's will is "good," in that it leads to our spiritual and moral well-being; it is "pleasing" insofar as it pleases God; and it is perfect, since we cannot amend or improve on the will of God.

2. This is an ongoing process (often a struggle) that cannot be completed easily or immediately. The "pattern of this world" knows nothing of the will of God, and to the extent that it conflicts with the will and plan of God, it is to be identified and avoided. This will not happen intuitively; such transformation involves "the renewing of your mind," which takes place by means of a constant interaction with the Holy Spirit working through the Word of God. On the basis of such renewal, one is in a position to "test and approve" what God's will is, for he or she can evaluate something on the basis of God's revealed and written expression of His will.

3. First, we notice how the chapter begins: Everything starts with the mercy of God. This means that the Gospel is central not only to everything that we do, but it also informs our relationships with each other as well. Throughout the rest of the chapter, the pattern is clear: We put the brother or sister in Christ—and his or her needs—first. We are called to a lifestyle of self-denial, and our pattern for such self-denial is our Lord Himself.

Closing

Follow the suggestion in the study guide.

Lesson 12

Submission and Love

The Class Session

Have volunteers read "Theme Verses," "Goal," and "What's Going On Here?"

Searching the Scriptures

1. The two reasons given for compliance are fear of punishment and one's own conscience, with the latter being a better motive than the former. An informed conscience recognizes that God has established government and works through it to accomplish His good purposes.

2. The Christian citizen will pray for those in authority and will give thanks for the blessings that come through it. He or she will be peaceable, considerate, and humble; eager to do what is good and right; and will slander no one (Titus 3:1–2). The Christian citizen will submit to every authority instituted by God. He or she will silence ignorance by doing good, live as a free person, use freedom responsibly, be a servant, show respect to everyone, and bring honor to his or her government (1 Peter 2:13). 1 Timothy 2:3 gives the reason for such behavior as bringing pleasure to God and enhancing the church's mission of bringing people to salvation.

3. Christians always recognize that their first loyalty or obedience is to God. Therefore, Christians will disobey the governing authorities whenever—but only whenever—they command them to do something that God has expressly forbidden.

4. Love is the fulfillment of the Law because God is love and because as an expression of His love He has accomplished our salvation. "We love because He first loved us" (1 John 4:19). Love is at the core of creation, at the center of God's choosing us to be His own, and at the heart of the Gospel—Jesus' life, sacrificial death, and resurrection. Therefore, love is the foundation of Christian ethics, relating to others as God in Christ has related to us.

5. In Ephesians 6:10–18 Paul refers to the spiritual armor Christians are to put on as truth, righteousness, the gospel of peace, faith, salvation, and the Word of God. The Holy Spirit equips us with this spiritual armor, which protects us from the assaults of the devil and his powers.

The Word for Us

1. Rulers abuse this text when they regard themselves as accountable to

no one, and forget that their power comes only from the hand of God (e.g., David, who ignored the fact that God had anointed him king over Israel [2 Samuel 12:7]). Failure to recognize that their power comes from God is the beginning of totalitarianism.

2. Being clothed with Christ is being dressed in the perfect righteousness of Christ through faith. This "clothing" first takes place in Baptism: "all of you who were baptized into Christ have clothed yourselves with Christ" (Galatians 3:27).

Closing

Follow the suggestion in the study guide.

Lesson 13

Living to the Lord

The Class Session

Have volunteers read "Theme Verses," "Goal," and "What's Going On Here?"

Searching the Scriptures

1. A dish of food or a day of the week is holy on the basis of the sanctified use to which it is put (1 Timothy 4:4–5). They are not matters about which one is to burden consciences or divide the church (Colossians 2:16–17). To make them such is to revert to a life under the Law and to forfeit the freedom Jesus Christ has won for us.

2. Our decisions regarding such indifferent matters as the observance of certain days and the eating of certain foods are made within the context of our relationship with the Lord. Each Christian seeks to honor the Lord, whom we love and serve. In response to His grace in Jesus Christ, we seek to give Him glory. Behind the phrase "to the Lord" is a determination to do certain things and to abstain from others. My decisions may not always be identical to those of other Christians; and my decisions, expressing a grace and faith relationship with the Lord, will have integrity.

3. The faith and spiritual well-being of a brother or sister in Christ is at stake in what we do and in how we react to misgivings about matters such as these. "Do not by your eating destroy your brother for whom Christ

died" (v. 15). Our principle, again, should be to "act in love." These matters should not divide the body of Christ. "For the kingdom of God is not a matter of eating and drinking, but of righteousness, peace and joy in the Holy Spirit, because anyone who serves Christ in this way is pleasing to God and approved by men" (vv. 17–18).

4. In verse 14 Paul exemplifies his effective leadership as he compliments and affirms his readers for their goodness, maturity, and competence. This kind of affirmation goes far to motivate the spiritual commitment of the Roman Christians. In 1 Corinthians 1:4–7 Paul assures his Corinthian readers that they have every spiritual gift necessary for effective Christian witness and ministry.

5. The collection for the poor of Jerusalem showed Paul's ongoing love and concern for his own people (recall chapters 9–11). For the Jews themselves, the collection provided real relief and also spoke of their inclusion as authentic members of the church. For the Gentile churches especially, the collection emphasized the oneness of the church, the centrality of giving, and the importance of the Jews and their heritage in the fellowship of believers.

6. The Gospel is nothing other than the proclamation of Jesus Christ. He is its message and content. The Gospel was revealed in the Old Testament (v. 26; see also especially Romans 1:2). The Old Testament as well as the New Testament contains the Gospel! The Gospel's scope is universal—"so that all nations might believe and obey Him." See also the Great Commission's reference to "all nations" in Matthew 28:19. The Gospel works faith, and it motivates love and obedience.

The Word for Us

1. While the lives of Christians will come to light in the judgment. Our sanctified lives give evidence of our faith and of the Holy Spirit's grace at work in us. But this judgment has nothing to do with our eternal destiny. Faith in Jesus Christ as one's personal Savior brings eternal salvation. Jesus, our Redeemer and Intercessor, bore our sin on the cross, conquered death at the empty tomb, and gives His righteousness to us.

2. The focus of our hope is God, who has provided salvation for us in Jesus Christ and continues to provide us with all good things.

3. Verse 7 spells out the Gospel motive ("just as Christ accepted you"), and verse 6 summarizes what such unity will enable us to do ("with one heart and mouth … glorify the God and Father of our Lord Jesus Christ"). In John 17, Jesus' high priestly prayer, our Lord prays for the oneness of His disciples and links that oneness to the successful conduct of their mission: "May they be brought to complete unity to let the world know that You sent Me and have loved them even as You have loved Me" (17:23).

Closing

Follow the suggestion in the study guide.